Living Aligned & Becoming CZND

Jalen Evers-Threatt

CONTENTS ▊

INTRODUCTION

PURPOSE OF THIS BOOK

We all strive for a better life—a life of clarity, purpose, confidence, and fulfillment. But to create that life, we first need to understand the **language** that shapes it. Words are not just definitions; they are frameworks, tools, and bridges between who we are now and who we are becoming.

This book is a *Lifestyle Development Dictionary: 300+ Terms to Know and Master to Enhance Your Life*, this is more than a glossary. This dictionary was created to serve as a guide for reshaping the language of growth. Too often, the words we use limit us, trapping us in old definitions of success, failure, strength, and struggle. Each term has been carefully selected to empower your personal and professional evolution across **mindset, health, fitness, finance, nutrition, education, and entrepreneurship**. By redefining these terms through a lens of empowerment and possibility, this dictionary provides a vocabulary for transformation. Its purpose is not just to explain words, but to shift mindsets—helping readers build clarity, resilience, and self-awareness on their personal journey of development. These words are the vocabulary of transformation—concepts that, when understood and embodied, can shift your perspective, elevate your habits, and unlock new levels of awareness and potential.

Whether you're a student of self-development, a coach, a creative, a business owner, or simply someone committed to becoming your best self, this dictionary offers clarity where there is confusion, and direction where there is drift.

PERSONAL STORY

There was a time when I felt like I had no control over my life—no matter how much willpower I had or how hard I tried to do what was "right." Looking back, I realize I only had ideas of how to improve my life, but no real method—from fitness and health, to skill development, to choosing the right career. Before I turned 25, I had worked 20–25 different jobs, searching for "the one for me." I decided entrepreneurship was the answer since I couldn't handle working for someone else. I was wrong. Success was minimal, but failure became my greatest teacher, showing me the areas I excelled at naturally.

Fitness, for example, was always part of me—maybe because of my ADHD and the need to burn energy, or perhaps from years of playing sports. I became a personal trainer to do what I loved, but even that lasted only a year or two. I still felt unfulfilled. Then COVID hit, testing my ability to persevere and innovate—tests I failed—forcing yet another pivot in my already unpredictable journey.

I felt like a leaf blown by the wind, drifting wherever life took me. I changed my major three times, dropped out of college repeatedly over nearly a decade, and juggled multiple career paths when I should have focused on one. In simple terms, I was undecided, undisciplined, and uncontrolled, carrying a doubtful mind, short-sighted vision, and fractured emotional regulation. I believed effort alone would create success. I let my environment, emotions, and doubts dictate my path. I procrastinated, and I waited for clarity that never came.

Everything began to change when I discovered the power of words. I became intentional about understanding terms I had previously taken for granted—reading definitions, exploring examples, and connecting them to my own life. I simplified their meanings into actionable concepts, turning abstract ideas into tools for growth. Mindset, for example, became my conscious choice of attitude and perspective, not just a buzzword.

I also realized that "superpowers" were not fantasy—they were mastery. Skills are words attached to action. If I could intentionally develop enough skills, I could create my own superpowers. This idea ignited a shift in me. I felt empowered, confident, and intentional about my journey for the first time.

This dictionary is the product of that shift. It is a method I used to learn, grow, and redefine myself. Now, I invite you to do the same: explore these words, make them your own, and use them to enhance your understanding of life. Live intentionally. Live aligned.

HOW TO USE IT

This dictionary is more than a collection of words—it's a tool for transformation. You can use it as a daily practice by choosing one word each day or week and reflecting on its meaning in your life, journaling about it, or setting an intention to live it out. Each definition can also serve as an affirmation, helping you reshape self-talk and shift perspective—turning "failure" into "feedback" or "discipline" into "self-respect."

Beyond personal reflection, this dictionary can guide group conversations, coaching sessions, or classroom discussions, offering language that sparks deeper dialogue around growth and values. It can also be used as a mindfulness tool, where a single word becomes the theme for meditation, visualization, or quiet focus. Whether you use it to align with your goals, reset your mindset in tough moments, or inspire your team or community, this resource is designed to be living and flexible—growing with you as you grow.

Read it once for inspiration. Return to it often for re-calibration. Master these terms, and you'll begin mastering the life you truly desire.

PRACTICES

Daily Word Practice : Pick a word each day/week to learn, align with your life, and to focus & practice on. Reflect on its meaning, journal about how you demonstrate it or how you can, and set an intention to live it out.

Affirmation Builder : Turn definitions into affirmations. Example - If the word is alignment, the affirmation could be "I align my thoughts, words, and actions with my highest values, trusting that when I move in harmony with my purpose, life flows with clarity and direction."

Establish Values & Principles : Accept highly favored terms and definitions as values to live by daily. Example - The term discipline, create a Value Statement or Affirmation "I honor discipline as a form of self-respect. It means showing up for myself, even when it's uncomfortable, and committing to long-term growth over short-term comfort." Then set a principle action - 1) I keep promises I make to myself. 2) I choose habits that reinforce the person I am becoming. Use these to guide your daily decision making.

Journaling & Reflection : Use each word as a journaling prompt: What does this word mean in my life right now? Are you leveraging it in your life? If so, rate yourself 1-10, explain how you can use it better.

Group Discussions : Use it in group discussions, workshops, or team meetings to spark deeper dialogue around values, mindset, and growth. Coaches, educators, or mentors can use the dictionary to teach concepts of self-awareness, resilience, and leadership. Groups can create a *shared dictionary of values* by reflecting on and adding to the terms. Great for nonprofits, companies, or clubs.

Mindset Reset : When stuck in negative self-talk, flip to a word that offers a new perspective. Deescalate yourself rather than feed into your heightened emotions. Example: Failing a test and looking up the definition of resilience. Create or find examples of resilience and motivate yourself to be resilient in this immediate moment for your next test or make up test.

Goal Alignment : Revisit key terms that connect to your personal or professional goals. Once understood, set a goal to be self-aware through the day/week and track how well you are aligning with that term. Ask: *How can I embody this word while working toward my vision? Example* - If the term is vision, once understanding the meaning, create a vision for yourself that you would feel good about. If my vision is to live a healthy, energized life, my fitness and nutrition goals must reflect that. Then transition to setting up goals around that vision.

Meditation/Mindfulness Guide : Focus on one word during meditation or quiet reflection. Let whatever thoughts, or feelings come to you revolving around that word. Block out any other thoughts during the period. Let it become a theme for your mediation session.

Creative Use : Add words and definitions into vision boards, journal margins, or artwork. If you are in any type of communication/expressive atmospheres, use these terms to implement your learned development into your outlets & outputs. Use them as captions, mantras, or personal motto's throughout discussions, social media posts, or content themes.

WHAT YOU'LL GAIN

Self-mastery → using the terms to define your ability to intentionally direct your thoughts, emotions, and actions in alignment with your highest values and goals. It means having control over your inner world rather than being controlled by impulses, external pressures, or limiting beliefs.

Self-Awareness → using the terms to understand and guide your thoughts, triggers, habits, and emotions.

Self-Discipline → using the terms to understand then have the ability to make consistent choices aligned with long-term vision, even when uncomfortable.

Emotional Regulation → managing feelings without suppressing them; responding rather than reacting.

Clarity of Purpose → knowing your "why" and using it as a compass.

Growth Mindset → treating challenges as opportunities to expand, not threats.

Self-mastery creates freedom: you're no longer a prisoner of old patterns.
- It builds resilience in the face of setbacks.
- It strengthens leadership, since leading others starts with leading yourself.
- It deepens fulfillment by aligning daily choices with a bigger purpose.

This dictionary is your companion for growth and clarity. Each word invites you to reflect, redefine, and act with intention. Use it to align your thoughts, choices, and values, and let it guide you toward a life of purpose, awareness, and empowered action.

LET'S BEGIN!!!

1

A

1.   **Alignment:** is the state of harmony between your values, vision, and actions. It means living in a way where your choices, habits, and goals reflect who you truly are and who you want to become.

Example - If my vision is to live a healthy and purposeful life, then alignment means not only saying I value health but also choosing nourishing foods, eating habits, committing to regular exercise, and making rest a priority. It means that when I set career goals, they are connected to my deeper purpose rather than just short-term gains.

2.   **Accountability:** is the commitment to take full ownership of my choices, actions, and results. It is not about blame or shame, but about responsibility—standing by my word and learning from the outcomes I create.

Example - If I set a goal to wake up at 6 a.m. to work on my craft but I oversleep, accountability means I acknowledge the slip, reflect on why it happened, and adjust my habits—rather than making excuses or pointing fingers. In relationships or work, it means being reliable, following through on promises, and openly communicating when challenges arise.

3. **Acceptance** – is the practice of acknowledging & embracing reality or yourself as it is, without denial, resistance, or judgment. It does not mean giving up or agreeing with everything—it means seeing clearly, embracing truth, and choosing how to respond with peace and intention.

    Example - If I face a setback at work, acceptance means acknowledging the disappointment without pretending it didn't happen or letting it define me. It allows me to say, "This is where I am now," and then decide my next step with clarity rather than frustration. In relationships, it means recognizing people for who they are, rather than who I wish they would be, including yourself.

4. **Action** – is the bridge between intention and outcome. It is the deliberate step taken to bring vision, ideas, and goals into reality. Without action, even the best plans remain only thoughts.

    Example - If I say I want to improve my health, action means scheduling workouts, preparing nourishing meals, and following through day by day. In personal growth, it means not just reading or learning, but applying the lessons in real situations. Action transforms "I want to" into "I am doing."

5. **Active Recovery:** is the practice of restoring energy and balance through intentional movement, mindfulness, and self-care. Unlike complete rest, it allows the body and mind to heal while staying engaged in light, purposeful activity.
    Example - After a demanding week of work, emotions, or intense exercise, active recovery may look like stretching, yoga, walking, journaling, or meditating. Instead of shutting down completely, I choose activities that refresh me while keeping momentum. In per-

sonal growth, it means taking time to reflect, reset, and recharge so I can return stronger and more focused.

6.   **Authenticity:** is the practice of living in alignment with who I truly am—my values, beliefs, and unique identity—without masking myself to meet external expectations. It is the courage to be genuine, even when vulnerability feels risky.

Example - If I value honesty, authenticity means expressing my truth with respect rather than hiding my feelings to please others. In my career, it means choosing paths that reflect my passions and strengths rather than chasing what looks good to others. Authenticity is showing up as the same person in private as I do in public.

7.   **Advocate:** is someone who actively supports, uplifts, or speaks on behalf of themselves or others. Advocacy is the practice of standing for a cause, idea, what is right, raising awareness, and creating pathways for change and empowerment in alignment with your values, whether for yourself, others, or a greater mission.

Example - To be my own advocate, I communicate my needs clearly, set healthy boundaries, and pursue opportunities that align with my values. To be an advocate for others, I listen to their voices, amplify their concerns, and take action to ensure fairness, inclusion, and justice—whether in my community, workplace, or relationships.

8.   **Ambition** – is the inner drive to pursue purpose, growth, and achievement beyond comfort. It is not just wanting more, but being willing to act, learn, and sacrifice in order to become more. True ambition aligns with values, fuels progress, and shapes goals and vision into reality.

Example - Ambition can look like setting a goal to finish a degree, start a business, or master a skill—and then committing to the daily steps that move me forward. It's choosing long-term fulfillment over short-term comfort. For example, instead of settling for a job that only pays the bills, ambition inspires me to pursue work that challenges me, develops my gifts, and builds the future I imagine.

9.   **Aspiration** – is the vision of who I want to become and what I hope to achieve. Unlike ambition, which is the drive and action toward achievement, skills-sets, or a better self, aspiration is the seed of inspiration—the dream, the ideal, the higher calling that guides my path.

Example - Aspiration can be imagining a future where I live with freedom, impact, and purpose. For example, I may aspire to become a leader who inspires others, a parent who raises children with wisdom, or an individual who contributes to meaningful change in the world. While ambition fuels the steps, aspiration paints the picture of the destination.

10.   **Appreciation** – is the practice of recognizing and valuing the positive aspects of life or other people, experiences, and blessings in life. It is more than saying "thank you"—it is choosing to see the worth, beauty, and significance in both the small and big things.

Example - Appreciation can look like pausing to acknowledge a friend's support, enjoying the present moment instead of rushing ahead, or reflecting on how far I've come in my journey. For example, even on difficult days, I can show appreciation by writing down three things I'm grateful for—whether it's my health, an opportu-

nity, or simply the sunrise.

11. **Affirmations:** are intentional, positive statements that reflect the truth I want to create in my life. They are tools to reshape my mindset, reinforce my values, and guide my negative thoughts toward growth, confidence, and purpose.

    Example - Using affirmations can look like starting the day by stating, "I am capable of growth and open to learning." Or when facing challenges, saying, "I trust myself to make choices that align with my highest vision." Repeating affirmations helps internalize beliefs, redirect self-talk, and strengthen intention.

12. **Awareness:** is the conscious recognition of my thoughts, emotions, behaviors, and surroundings through the interconnectedness of the past, future, and present. It is the ability to observe without judgment, understand patterns, and respond intentionally rather than react impulsively.

    Example - Awareness can look like noticing when stress is influencing your decisions, recognizing the emotions behind a conflict, or identifying habits that no longer serve your growth. For example, if I feel frustrated during a conversation, awareness allows me to pause, reflect on why I feel this way, and choose a measured response instead of reacting impulsively.

13. **Asset (to one's life) :** is anything in my life—skill, mindset, person, quality, habit, relationship, or resource—that adds value, strengthens my growth, or supports my long-term goals enriching my overall well-being. Assets are tools I can leverage to create opportunities, overcome challenges, and build the life I desire.

    Example - A skill like public speaking can be an asset if I use it to in-

spire others or advance my career. A strong friendship can be an asset when it provides support and perspective during difficult times. Even habits like discipline, consistency, and time management are intangible assets that compound over time to create meaningful results.

14.   **Asset Allocation:** is the intentional distribution of resources—skills, time, energy, and money—across areas of life to maximize growth, balance, and long-term success. It is about investing wisely in what matters most and diversifying efforts to avoid over-reliance on a single area. A strategy that balances risk and reward by dividing assets.

Example - If I have limited time in a day, I allocate it intentionally: dedicating mornings to learning and skill development, afternoons to work or business projects, and evenings to relationships, health, or rest. Similarly, in finances, I might distribute funds across savings, investments, and personal development. The goal is to ensure my resources support multiple aspects of a fulfilled life rather than being concentrated in just one area.

2

B

1. **Balance**: is the conscious practice of distributing energy, attention, and effort across the areas of life that matter most. The ability to maintain harmony across different areas of life (work, health, relationships, etc. It is not perfection or equal time for everything, but harmony that supports well-being, growth, and fulfillment.

   Example - Balance can look like managing work, health, relationships, and personal growth without neglecting any one area for too long. For example, I may dedicate mornings to focused work, afternoons to exercise or learning, and evenings to family and rest. Balance also includes knowing when to push forward and when to pause, allowing recovery and reflection.

2. **Belief**: is the conviction or mental acceptance and trust in a thought, idea, or principle as true, which shapes perception,thoughts, emotions, choices, and behavior. It acts as the lens through which I interpret experiences and guide my actions.

   Example - If I believe that persistence leads to growth, I will keep taking steps toward my goals even when progress feels slow. In relationships, believing in people's potential can shape how I interact, support, and communicate with them. Beliefs can empower or limit me, depending on whether they serve my growth or hold me back.

3. **Belief System:** is a collection of interconnected beliefs that shape how I perceive the world, make decisions, and respond to experiences. It forms the foundation of my values, thoughts, habits, and identity, guiding my thoughts, emotions, and actions.

   Example - If my belief system values growth, resilience, and integrity, I am likely to approach challenges as opportunities, remain persistent in the face of setbacks, and make choices that align with my principles. Conversely, a limiting belief system—one that prioritizes fear, scarcity, or judgment—can constrain my potential and create self-imposed barriers.

4. **Belonging**: is the feeling of acceptance, values, connection, and alignment within a community, environment, or relationship. It is the awareness that you are seen, valued, and supported for who you truly are.

   Example - Belonging can look like contributing your unique voice in a team, feeling safe to share your ideas without judgment, or being part of a group that celebrates your individuality while valuing collective growth. It also includes self-belonging—accepting and honoring yourself as worthy of connection and inclusion.

5. **Benefit**: is a positive outcome, advantage, or gain that comes from an action, choice, relationship, or experience. Benefits can be tangible or intangible, immediate or long-term, and they contribute to growth, well-being, or value in life.

   Example - Exercising regularly provides the benefit of improved health, increased energy, and mental clarity. Learning a new skill brings the benefit of confidence, expanded opportunities, and personal growth. Even challenges carry benefits, such as resilience and wisdom gained from overcoming obstacles.

6. **Bloom's Taxonomy:** is a hierarchical model & framework for learning and thinking that categorizes cognitive skills from basic to advanced levels. It helps structure knowledge acquisition, critical thinking, and mastery by progressing through stages: remembering, understanding, applying, analyzing, evaluating, and creating.

*Example - If I want to learn a new skill, I start by **remembering** the basic concepts, then **understand** how they work, **apply** them in practice, **analyze** patterns or problems, **evaluate** effectiveness, and finally **create** something new using what I've learned. For example, learning public speaking could follow this path: memorize key principles → understand audience engagement → practice delivering speeches → analyze feedback → refine techniques → create original presentations.*

7. **Boundaries:** are the healthy limits and rules I set to protect my energy, mental & emotional spaces, values, and well-being. They define what I will accept, how I allow others to treat me, and how I manage my time, emotions, and relationships.

Example - Boundaries can look like saying no to requests that drain your energy, limiting time with people who create stress, or clearly communicating expectations in relationships. For example, if a colleague repeatedly interrupts your focus, setting a boundary may mean politely stating that you need uninterrupted work time and scheduling a time to discuss questions later. Healthy boundaries create space for growth, respect, and emotional balance.

8. **Bravery:** is the willingness to face fear, uncertainty, or discomfort with courage and intention in pursuit of growth or truth. It

is not the absence of fear, but the choice to act despite it, guided by values and purpose.

Example - Bravery can look like speaking up for what is right even when it's unpopular, pursuing a dream despite risk of failure, or confronting personal challenges that feel intimidating. For example, sharing a difficult truth with a friend or mentor requires bravery, as does stepping into a leadership role that pushes you beyond your comfort zone.

9.   **Breakthrough**: is a sudden or significant shift in understanding, performance, or perspective that propels growth, change, and opens new possibilities. It often comes after persistent effort, reflection, or overcoming obstacles.

Example - A breakthrough can look like realizing a limiting belief is holding you back and choosing a new mindset, mastering a skill after months of practice, or finding clarity in a complex problem that unlocks your next steps. For example, after struggling with procrastination, a breakthrough might occur when you develop a system that allows consistent focus, dramatically improving productivity and confidence.

10.   **Breakthrough Thinking**: is the innovative thinking and mindset of seeking solutions, opportunities, and growth beyond perceived limitations. It involves breaking away from conventional patterns to solve problems or unlock growth, questioning assumptions, embracing challenges, and viewing obstacles as stepping stones rather than barriers. (Process leading to a breakthrough and a mindset/mentality enabled.)

Example - If I face a career setback, breakthrough thinking means asking not "Why did this happen to me?" but "What can I learn, and how can I pivot to create new opportunities?" In personal growth, it's choosing to explore unconventional strategies, experiment with new habits, and continuously adapt. For example, instead of giving up on a stalled project, I brainstorm alternative approaches, seek feedback, and refine my plan until I move forward successfully.

11. **Building**: is the intentional act of creating, developing, or strengthening something over time. The ongoing process of creating or improving can apply to aspects like skills, habits, relationships, knowledge, or personal growth, and emphasizes consistent effort and progress.

Example - Building can look like developing a new skill through daily practice, cultivating strong relationships through trust and communication, or growing a business step by step. For example, consistently dedicating time to exercise builds physical health, while daily journaling builds self-awareness and clarity.

12. **Burnout**: is a state of physical, mental, or emotional exhaustion caused by prolonged stress, overwork, or imbalance. It reduces motivation, productivity, and well-being, signaling a need for rest, reflection, and realignment.

Example - Burnout can look like feeling constantly drained, losing interest in work or activities once enjoyed, struggling to focus, or experiencing irritability and frustration with little provocation. For example, someone pushing themselves to meet constant deadlines without adequate rest or self-care may eventually hit a point where their body and mind can no longer sustain effort effectively.

13. **Body Composition:** refers to the proportion of fat, muscle, bone, and other tissues in the body. It is a more meaningful mea-

sure of health and fitness than weight alone, as it reflects the balance between lean mass and fat mass.

Example - Improving body composition can look like increasing muscle through strength training while reducing excess body fat through proper nutrition and activity. For example, someone might track their progress not just by scale weight but by how their clothes fit, strength gains, or body fat percentage, focusing on building a stronger, healthier body rather than just losing weight.

14. **Biofeedback :** is the practice of using real-time data from the body—such as heart rate, muscle tension, or brain activity—to increase awareness and control over physiological processes. It helps improve health, performance, and emotional regulation by making invisible signals visible.

Example - Biofeedback can look like using a heart rate monitor to notice stress spikes during work and then practicing deep breathing to calm the nervous system. It could also involve tracking muscle tension to improve posture, or using meditation apps that provide feedback on brainwave patterns to enhance focus and relaxation. By observing and responding to these signals, I can regulate my body and mind more effectively.

3

C

1. **Clarity:** is the state of being mentally clear and focused in thought, intention, and purpose. It allows me to see situations, choices, and goals without confusion, distraction, or distortion, enabling confident and aligned action enabling sharpness and understanding.

    Example - Clarity can look like taking time to reflect before making a decision, organizing priorities to understand what truly matters, or articulating a vision for the future that guides daily actions. For example, before committing to a new project, I gain clarity by evaluating whether it aligns with my values, goals, and available resources.

    1. **Cognitive Bias:** is a systematic pattern of deviation or mental shortcut that can distort thinking and affect perception, judgment, and decision-making. It occurs when the brain processes information in a way that is influenced by assumptions, emotions, or past experiences rather than objective reality.

        Example - One common cognitive bias is the confirmation bias, where I focus only on information that supports my existing beliefs and ignore evidence that challenges them. For example, if I believe I'm "bad at public speaking," I might only remember times I stumbled, while forgetting times I spoke confidently, reinforcing a false narrative. Awareness of cognitive biases allows me to think more objectively and make better decisions.

2.   **Confidence:** is the belief in one's abilities, judgment, and capacity to take action. It is a sense of self-assurance that allows me to trust and face challenges, make decisions, and pursue goals with courage and clarity amidst acknowledging ones worth.

Example : Confidence can look like speaking up in a meeting, sharing my ideas with others, or tackling a project that feels challenging without fear of failure. For example, if I've prepared for a presentation, confidence allows me to deliver it effectively, trust my knowledge, and handle questions with composure. Confidence grows through experience, preparation, and consistent action.

3.   **Core Beliefs:** are the fundamental deep-seated views and convictions I hold about myself, others, and the world. They shape my perceptions, decisions, behaviors, and emotional responses, forming the foundation of my mindset.

Example - Believing I am capable of growth encourages me to embrace challenges as opportunities, while a limiting belief like I'm not enough may cause hesitation or self-doubt.

4.   **Courage:** is the ability to act despite fear, uncertainty, or discomfort. It involves stepping into vulnerability and taking action aligned with my values.

Example - Courage can look like confronting difficult conversations, starting a new venture, or speaking my truth even when it feels risky.

5. **Critical Thinking:** is the ability to analyze information objectively, evaluate evidence, and make reasoned decisions without bias or assumption.

    Example - Before accepting advice or news, I evaluate the source, check facts, and consider alternative perspectives to make informed decisions.

6. **Cognitive Load:** is the total amount of mental effort being used in working memory. Managing cognitive load helps maintain focus, learning, and productivity.

    Example - Breaking complex tasks into smaller steps or reducing distractions lightens cognitive load, making it easier to process information and make decisions.

7. **Compounding:** The process by which small, consistent actions, habits,gains or decisions build upon one another over time and accumulate, creating exponential growth and significant results in personal, emotional, physical, or professional areas of life.

    Example - Reading 20 pages a day compounds into multiple books per year, and small daily investments grow into substantial wealth over time.

8. **Compound Interest:** The cumulative benefit or return gained from repeatedly investing time, energy, or intention into self-improvement, where progress multiplies not just from the action itself, but from the growth those actions create over time.

Example – Learning one new skill each year not only adds knowledge but also expands opportunities, creating a snowball effect where each skill builds on the last, multiplying personal and professional growth over time.

10.   **Credit:** The recognition, trust, or reputation earned through consistent integrity, reliability, and contribution to others or the community.

Example – Paying bills on time builds financial credit, while consistently showing up for friends builds personal credit in relationships.

11.   **Circadian Rhythm:** The natural, internal process that regulates the sleep-wake cycle and repeats roughly every 24 hours, impacting energy, focus, and overall health.

Example – Going to bed and waking up at the same time daily aligns with your circadian rhythm, improving sleep quality and daytime productivity.

12.   **Commitment**: A firm dedication to a goal, value, or path despite challenges or setbacks, representing persistence and loyalty to one's intentions.

Example – Training daily for a marathon, even in unfavorable weather, shows commitment to the goal of finishing the race.

13.   **Consistency**: The repeated application of behaviors or habits that support long-term success, creating reliability and stability in results.

Example – Practicing an instrument for 30 minutes every day leads to steady improvement over time through consistency.

14. **Compassion**: The ability to empathize with others while extending kindness, understanding, and support, often inspiring healing and connection.

Example – Listening to a friend in distress without judgment demonstrates compassion in action.

15. **Curiosity**: A strong desire to learn, explore, or understand yourself, others, or the world, driving discovery and growth.

Example – Asking questions in class or experimenting with new hobbies reflects curiosity that fuels personal development.

16. **Challenge**:A test, obstacle, or difficult circumstance that, when faced with effort and resilience, promotes growth and strength.

Example – Tackling a tough project at work may be a challenge, but overcoming it builds confidence and skill.

17. **Contribution**: The act of giving time, energy, or value to something greater than yourself, creating impact and significance.

Example – Volunteering at a food bank is a contribution that directly benefits the community.

18. **Creativity**: The ability to think outside the box, connect ideas, and generate new, meaningful solutions or expressions.

Example – Designing a unique business logo or writing a poem are acts of creativity at work.

19. **Consciousness**:An elevated state of awareness regarding your thoughts, emotions, and behaviors, allowing intentional choices and growth.

Example – Pausing to notice negative self-talk and replacing it with affirmations reflects a higher level of consciousness.

4

D

1. **Digital Literacy & Exploration:** The ability to effectively navigate, understand, evaluate, and create using digital tools and technologies, paired with the curiosity and initiative to explore new platforms, skills, and digital environments. This combination empowers individuals to think critically, communicate effectively, and continuously grow in a connected, tech-driven world.

    Example – Learning to design presentations, use AI tools, and explore coding platforms builds digital literacy and exploration that keeps you adaptable in a fast-changing world.

2. **Diversification:** The practice of expanding your skills, experiences, habits, and perspectives across different areas of life to enhance adaptability, resilience, and overall growth. Just as in nature or learning, variety strengthens you—helping you navigate change, avoid burnout, and uncover new opportunities for success and fulfillment.

    Example – Balancing physical fitness, financial education, and creative hobbies creates diversification that strengthens multiple areas of life at once.

3. **Daily Routine:** Consistent structure of activities done daily for productivity and growth.

Example – Starting your day with exercise, journaling, and reviewing your goals builds a daily routine that fuels focus and success.

4. **Discipline** – The ability to stay focused and consistent in actions that align with your goals.

Example – Sticking to a study plan every night, even when you're tired, reflects discipline in pursuit of long-term achievement.

5. **Determination** – Persistent effort and mental resolve to overcome obstacles and achieve growth.

Example – Training through setbacks to eventually finish a marathon demonstrates determination to succeed despite challenges.

6. **Development** – The process of evolving in knowledge, behavior, or lifestyle.

Example – Taking new courses and practicing better communication skills represent development in both career and relationships.

7. **Direction** – A sense of purposeful movement toward a desired outcome or vision.

Example – Choosing a career path aligned with your passions gives you direction in how you spend your time and energy.

8.   **Drive** – Inner motivation or energy that pushes you to take action and pursue improvement.

Example – Waking up early to work on a business idea before your regular job shows drive to achieve more.

9.   **Decision** – A conscious choice that shapes your future through intentional action.

Example – Deciding to save money instead of spending impulsively sets you on a path to financial stability.

10.   **Dedication** – Wholehearted commitment to a cause, goal, or personal value.

Example – Practicing daily for years to master a musical instrument is dedication in action.

11.   **Detachment** – The practice of letting go of unhealthy attachments to outcomes, people, or expectations.

Example – Focusing on doing your best without obsessing over what others think is practicing detachment.

12.   **Discovery** – The process of finding new insights about yourself, others, or the world.

Example – Traveling to new places and meeting people from different cultures leads to discovery that expands your perspective.

Daring – Boldness to take risks or step outside your comfort zone for the sake of growth.

Example – Speaking up with a new idea in a meeting, even if uncertain of others' reactions, is an act of daring

5

E

1. **Elevation** – The act of rising others or yourself to a higher level of consciousness, behavior, purpose or lifestyle.

   Example – Encouraging a friend to pursue their goals instead of settling for less is an act of elevation.

2. **Energy** – The physical or mental vitality required for action, focus, and sustained growth.

   Example – Eating healthy and exercising daily provides the energy needed to stay productive and creative throughout the day.

3. **Enlightenment** – A deep understanding or awakening that leads to personal transformation.

   Example – Realizing the importance of self-love before seeking validation from others is a moment of enlightenment.

4. **Endurance** – The ability to sustain effort and commitment over time, especially through difficulties.

   Example – Training consistently for months to finish a long-distance race demonstrates endurance.

5. **Engagement** – Active participation and emotional investment in what matters to you.

Example – Asking questions in class and contributing to group projects shows engagement in learning.

6. **Execution** – Turning plans or ideas into action with intention and follow-through.

Example – Writing and publishing your first blog post after weeks of planning shows execution at work.

7. **Expansion** – The act of growing beyond current limits in mindset, habits, or environment.

Example – Learning a new language to connect with more people reflects expansion of personal horizons.

8. **Excellence** – The pursuit of quality and high standards in your thoughts, actions, or results.

Example – Double-checking your work to ensure accuracy demonstrates excellence in practice.

9. **Emotional Conditioning:** Patterns of emotional response developed over time.

Example – Remaining calm under criticism after years of practicing mindfulness reflects emotional conditioning.

10. **Emotional Intelligence:** Ability to identify, manage, and express emotions effectively.

Example – Noticing when a teammate feels stressed and offering encouragement demonstrates emotional intelligence.

11.   **Empowerment:** The process of gaining control, confidence, and equipped with the tools to make meaningful life choices and control over your life

Example – Learning financial literacy empowers you to manage money wisely and achieve independence.

12.   **Equanimity:** Calmness and balance, especially under stress.

Example – Responding with patience instead of anger during an argument reflects equanimity.

6

F

1. **Fixed Mindset:** Belief that your abilities, talents, and intelligence are unchangeable.

    Example – Avoiding new challenges because you think you're "not good at math" reflects a fixed mindset.

2. **Freelancing:** Working for oneself rather than for a company.

    Example – A graphic designer taking on projects from multiple businesses is freelancing instead of working a 9–5 job.

3. **Forgiveness:** The conscious decision to release resentment or blame for the sake of inner peace. Letting go of resentment toward yourself or others.

    Example – Choosing to forgive a friend who made a mistake allows the relationship to move forward with trust.

4. **Functional Training:** Exercises that train the body for activities in daily life

    Example – Practicing squats helps with everyday movements like lifting groceries or standing up from a chair.

1. **Focus**: Concentrated attention on what matters most to achieve clarity and results.

    Example – Turning off notifications to study for an exam shows focus on your priority task.

2. **Fulfillment**: A deep sense of satisfaction and purpose from meaningful experiences or accomplishments.

    Example – Volunteering to help others often brings a feeling of fulfillment that money alone cannot provide.

3. **Flexibility**: The ability to adapt thoughts, behaviors, or plans in response to change or challenge.

    Example – Shifting to remote work smoothly during unexpected circumstances demonstrates flexibility.

4. **Faith**: Belief in something greater—whether yourself, a goal, or a higher purpose—even without immediate proof.

    Example – Continuing to build your business despite setbacks shows faith in your long-term success.

5. **Flow**: A mental state of full immersion and engagement in an activity where time seems to disappear.

    Example – A writer who becomes completely absorbed in drafting a novel is experiencing flow.

6. **Freedom**: The power to make choices aligned with your values, desires, and authenticity.

Example – Choosing to travel the world while working remotely represents freedom to live on your own terms.

7.   **Fuel**: Anything (mental, emotional, physical, or spiritual) that energizes or motivates you to grow.

Example – Listening to motivational podcasts before starting your day can serve as fuel for productivity.

8.   **Foundation**: The base or core principles, habits, and values that support a thriving lifestyle.

Example – A foundation of discipline and consistency helps an athlete prepare for championship success.

9.   **Fearlessness**: Moving forward despite fear, uncertainty, or doubt in pursuit of progress.

Example – Speaking in front of a large audience for the first time shows fearlessness in pursuing growth.

7

G

1. **Growth Assessment:** Evaluation of progress over time rather than performance at a single point.

    Example – Comparing how many books you've read this year versus last year is a growth assessment that shows long-term development.

2. **Gratitude:** Acknowledging and Appreciating the positive aspects of life and cultivating a mindset of thankfulness.

    Example – Writing down three things you're grateful for each morning helps build gratitude and positivity.

3. **Grit:** Sustained effort, interest, perseverance and passion for long-term goals despite obstacles and setbacks.

    Example – A student who keeps studying and retaking exams until they pass demonstrates grit.

4. **Growth**: The process of developing skills, mindset, and habits to become a better version of yourself.

    Example – Learning to manage stress more effectively over time shows personal growth.

5. **Growth Mindset:** Belief that skills, intelligence, and abilities can be developed through dedication and hard work.

Example – Viewing mistakes as lessons instead of failures reflects a growth mindset.

6. **Goals**: Clear, specific objectives that guide your actions and measure progress.

Example – Setting a goal to run 5 miles within three months gives structure and motivation to training.

7. **Goal Setting:** Process of identifying something you want to achieve and setting a plan.

Example – Breaking down the goal of starting a business into smaller steps like creating a budget, registering an LLC, and launching a website is goal setting in practice.

8. **Generosity**: The willingness to give time, energy, or resources to others without expecting anything in return.

Example – Offering to tutor a classmate for free is an act of generosity.

9. **Grounding**: Techniques or practices that help you stay present, centered, and connected to the moment.

Example – Taking deep breaths and noticing your surroundings when anxious is a grounding practice.

10. **Giving**: Acts of kindness or contribution that enrich your life and the lives of others.

Example – Donating clothes to a local shelter is giving that supports your community.

11.   **Gentleness**: Approaching yourself and others with kindness, patience, and care.

Example – Speaking calmly to a child after they make a mistake demonstrates gentleness.

12.   **Guidance**: Support, advice, or mentorship that helps you navigate growth and challenges.

Example – A coach offering feedback to improve your performance provides guidance.

13. **Genuineness**: Being honest, authentic, and transparent in your actions and interactions.

Example – Admitting when you don't know something instead of pretending shows genuineness.

8

H

1.   **Hypertrophy:** Increase in muscle size by exercise.

Example – Doing progressive weightlifting consistently leads to hypertrophy, making muscles larger and stronger.

2.   **Hydration:** Maintaining adequate fluid balance in the body.

Example – Drinking water regularly throughout the day keeps your body hydrated and improves focus and energy.

3.   **Heart Rate Variability:** Measurement of the variation in time between heartbeats; an indicator of stress.

Example – Tracking HRV daily can show how well your body recovers from workouts or stress.

4.   **Habits**: Regular behaviors or routines that shape your daily life and outcomes.

Example – Brushing teeth every morning and night is a simple habit that promotes oral health.

5.   **Healing**: The process of recovering emotionally, mentally, or physically from pain or injury.

Example – Practicing mindfulness and therapy after a stressful event supports emotional healing.

6.   **Habit Stacking:** Attaching a new habit to an existing one for easier adoption.

Example – Doing 10 push-ups immediately after brushing your teeth is a form of habit stacking.

7.   **Humility**: The quality of being modest and open to learning from others.

Example – Asking for feedback at work instead of assuming you're perfect demonstrates humility.

8.   **Happiness**: A state of well-being and contentment with life.

Example – Spending quality time with loved ones can increase your sense of happiness.

9.   **Health**: The overall condition of your body and mind, essential for thriving.

Example – Eating balanced meals, exercising, and sleeping well all contribute to long-term health.

10.   **Hope**: Expectation and desire for positive outcomes in the future.

Example – Believing you can recover from a setback and continue pursuing goals reflects hope.

11.   **Honesty**: Being truthful with yourself and others. (Free from deceit)

Example – Admitting a mistake to your team instead of hiding it demonstrates honesty.

12. **Harmony**: A balanced and peaceful state in relationships and within yourself.

Example – Resolving conflicts calmly at home fosters harmony with loved ones.

13. **Heartfulness**: Approaching life with kindness, empathy, and emotional openness.

Example – Listening fully to someone's struggles without judgment is an act of heartfulness.

14. **Hardiness**: Mental resilience and toughness in the face of stress or adversity.

Example – Staying focused on your work despite personal challenges demonstrates hardiness.

9

1.   **Innovation:**The creation or adoption of new ideas, methods, or products to improve life.

   Example – Designing a reusable water bottle that tracks hydration is an act of innovation.

2.   **Intrapreneurship:** Acting like an entrepreneur within a large organization (Ex.Family)

   Example – Suggesting a new family budget system to improve finances demonstrates intrapreneurship within your household.

3.   **Intermittent Fasting:** Eating pattern that cycles between periods of eating and fasting.

   Example – Skipping breakfast and eating within an 8-hour window each day is a form of intermittent fasting.

4.   **Identity:** Your self-concept, shaped by experience, beliefs, and roles.

   Example – Seeing yourself as a lifelong learner and creative thinker forms part of your identity.

5.   **Imposter Syndrome:** The feeling of being a fraud despite evidence of success.

Example – Believing you only got a promotion due to luck, not your skill, reflects imposter syndrome.

6. **Inner Child:** The emotional self formed in early childhood that still influences you.

   Example – Feeling nervous about speaking up in groups because of past criticism reflects your inner child's influence.

7. **Inner Dialogue:** The ongoing internal conversation with yourself.

   Example – Encouraging yourself before a presentation is a positive inner dialogue.

8. **Introspection:** Looking inward to examine your thoughts and feelings.

   Example – Reflecting on why a certain situation made you angry is introspection in practice.

9. **Intuition:** The ability to understand or know something instinctively, without conscious reasoning.

   Example – Choosing a career path based on a strong gut feeling demonstrates intuition.

10. **Intention** – A purposeful commitment or focus directing your thoughts and actions.

    Example – Setting an intention to practice gratitude daily guides your behavior and mindset.

11.   **Integrity** – Consistency between your values, words, and actions; honesty and moral uprightness.

Example – Returning money you accidentally received reflects integrity in action.

12.   **Insight** – A deep understanding or realization about yourself or a situation.

Example – Realizing that procrastination stems from fear rather than laziness is an insight.

13.   **Inspiration** – The process of being mentally stimulated to do or feel something meaningful.

Example – Watching a mentor overcome challenges can provide inspiration to pursue your own goals.

14.   **Influence** – The ability to affect others' thoughts, feelings, or actions positively.

Example – Sharing helpful habits that motivate your friends to improve their routines demonstrates influence.

15.   **Investment** – Committing time, energy, or resources toward growth or goals.

Example – Spending an hour every day learning a new language is an investment in your future skills.

16. **Inclusion** – Creating an environment where everyone feels valued and respected.

Example – Ensuring all team members are heard during a group project reflects inclusion.

13. **Imagination** – The ability to visualize possibilities beyond current reality.

Example – Dreaming up a new business concept that solves a common problem uses imagination.

10

J

1. **Journaling:** The practice of writing down thoughts, feelings, and experiences for reflection and growth regularly.

   Example – Writing about your daily challenges and successes each night helps you process emotions and track progress.

2. **Joy** – A deep feeling of happiness, pleasure, or delight that comes from within.

   Example – Feeling joy while playing music or spending time with loved ones reflects an internal state of happiness.

3. **Journey** – The ongoing process of growth, learning, and self-discovery.

   Example – Pursuing a career while continuously learning and improving represents a journey of personal development.

4. **Judgment** – The ability to make considered decisions or form sensible opinions.

   Example – Choosing the best solution for a problem after evaluating all options demonstrates good judgment.

5. **Juxtaposition** – Placing contrasting ideas or experiences side by side to gain new perspectives.

Example – Comparing successes and failures in your past projects can reveal patterns and lessons through juxtaposition.

6.   **Justice** – Fairness and equity in treatment and opportunities.

Example – Ensuring everyone in a team has an equal chance to speak and contribute demonstrates justice.

7.   **Joining** – The act of connecting or aligning with others or communities for mutual support.

Example – Joining a mastermind group helps you learn, grow, and share experiences with like-minded people.

8.   **Jumpstart** – An initial boost or motivation to begin a new habit, project, or phase.

Example – Setting a 7-day challenge to exercise daily jumpstarts a long-term fitness routine.

9.   **Justification** – The reasoning behind actions, beliefs, or decisions.

Example – Explaining why you chose a certain career path shows justification for your decision-making.

11

K

1. **Kindness** – The quality of being friendly, generous, and considerate toward yourself and others.

    Example – Offering support to a friend in need or speaking gently to yourself during a tough day demonstrates kindness.

2. **Knowledge** – Information, understanding, and skills gained through experience or education.

    Example – Learning financial literacy gives you knowledge to make smarter money decisions.

3. **Karma** – The spiritual principle of cause and effect where your actions influence your future.

    Example – Helping others without expecting anything in return can bring positive experiences later, reflecting good karma.

4. **Keystone Habit** – A foundational habit that leads to the development of other positive behaviors.

    Example – Exercising regularly as a keystone habit can lead to better eating, improved sleep, and increased productivity.

5. **Kickstart** – The initial energy or motivation to begin a new goal or process.

Example – Attending a workshop to jumpstart your personal growth routine provides a kickstart to consistent action.

6. **Keeping Boundaries** – Maintaining healthy limits in relationships and personal space.

Example – Saying no to extra work to preserve family time is an example of keeping boundaries.

7. **Kinetic Energy** – The energy of movement, often related metaphorically to taking action.

Example – Starting a small project and building momentum daily creates kinetic energy toward long-term success.

8. **Kaizen**: A Japanese term meaning *"continuous improvement."* It refers to the practice of making small, consistent, and incremental changes over time to improve performance, productivity, or quality—whether in life, work, health, or mindset.

Example – Improving your morning routine by adding one positive habit each week is practicing kaizen.

9. **Kindling** – Small sparks or moments that ignite passion, creativity, or motivation.

Example – Reading an inspiring book can act as kindling for new ideas or projects

10. **Knowledge Sharing** – The practice of exchanging information or skills for mutual growth.

Example – Teaching a colleague a new software shortcut is knowledge sharing.

11. **Knack** – A natural talent or skill for doing something well.

Example – Someone with a knack for storytelling easily engages and captivates an audience.

12

L

1. **Locus of Control:** Belief about whether outcomes are controlled by yourself or external forces.

   Example – Believing you can improve your health through consistent exercise reflects an internal locus of control.

2. **Lifelong Learning:** Continual, voluntary pursuit of knowledge for personal or professional growth.

   Example – Taking online courses to learn new skills even after finishing formal education demonstrates lifelong learning.

3. **Learning** – The ongoing process of acquiring knowledge, skills, or behaviors.

   Example – Practicing a musical instrument daily represents learning in action.

4. **Learning Styles:** Different approaches to or ways of learning.

   Example – A visual learner may benefit from diagrams, while a kinesthetic learner prefers hands-on practice.

5. **Leadership:** The ability to guide, inspire, and influence others positively.

Example – A team captain encouraging teammates to do their best while modeling discipline demonstrates leadership.

6.   **Lean Startup:** Methodology for developing businesses and products through experimentation.

Example – Launching a minimal version of an app to test user interest before fully developing it illustrates the lean startup approach.

7.   **Letting Go** – The act of releasing attachments, grudges, or limiting beliefs that no longer serve you.

Example – Forgiving past mistakes and moving forward reflects the practice of letting go.

8.   **Listening** – Actively paying attention to understand others and yourself better.

Example – Fully focusing on a friend's story without interrupting demonstrates effective listening.

9.   **Limitations** – Recognizing boundaries or obstacles that can be overcome or managed.

Example – Understanding that you need more practice to improve at public speaking acknowledges limitations while planning growth.

10.   **Love** – A profound feeling of care, connection, and compassion for yourself and others.

Example – Supporting a friend through hard times reflects love in action.

11.   **Luck** – The occurrence of positive events by chance or opportunity.

Example – Meeting a mentor at a random networking event could be considered luck, especially when combined with readiness to learn.

12.   **Lightness** – A state of ease, playfulness, and freedom from heavy burdens or stress.

Example – Laughing and enjoying a spontaneous adventure creates a sense of lightness in life.

13

M

1. **Mentality:** A habitual or characteristic way of thinking.

    Example – Approaching challenges with a "problem-solving" mentality helps you find solutions rather than get stuck.

2. **Metacognition:** Awareness and understanding of your own thought processes.

    Example – Reflecting on why you procrastinate before starting a project demonstrates metacognition.

3. **Mindfulness:** The practice of being fully present and aware of the moment without judgment.

    Example – Focusing on your breath during a stressful situation helps you respond mindfully instead of reacting impulsively.

4. **Mindset Shift:** A change in your core beliefs or thinking patterns.

    Example – Moving from "I can't do this" to "I can learn and improve" is a mindset shift toward growth.

5. **Mentorship:** Guidance and support provided by a more experienced person.

Example – Meeting regularly with a senior colleague to improve your skills demonstrates mentorship.

6. **Metabolic Conditioning:** Exercise protocols that improve the efficiency of the energy pathways.

Example – Circuit training that combines strength and cardio exercises enhances metabolic conditioning.

7. **Mobility:** Ability to move freely and easily through a full range of motion

Example – Stretching and foam rolling daily improves joint mobility and reduces risk of injury.

8. **Mental Flexibility:** It's your mind's ability to adjust, pivot, and grow when life throws something unexpected your way.

Example – Quickly adapting to a last-minute change in a project plan demonstrates mental flexibility.

9. **Macronutrients:** Nutrients required in large amounts: carbohydrates, proteins, and fats.

Example – Balancing macronutrients in meals supports energy, muscle growth, and overall health.

10. **Micronutrients:** Vitamins and minerals needed in small amounts for proper body function.

Example – Consuming fruits and vegetables ensures sufficient micronutrients like vitamin C and potassium.

11.   **Motivation** – The internal drive that initiates, guides, and sustains goal-directed behavior.

Example – Feeling excited to finish a project because it aligns with your career goals reflects motivation.

12.   **Mastery** – Comprehensive knowledge or skill in a particular area achieved through practice.

Example – Years of playing piano and refining technique leads to mastery of the instrument.

13.   **Meditation** – A technique to calm the mind and cultivate focused awareness.

Example – Sitting quietly and focusing on your breath for 10 minutes daily is a meditation practice.

14.   **Momentum** – The driving force gained by the development of a process or course of events.

Example – Exercising daily builds momentum that makes sticking to fitness goals easier over time.

15.   **Meaning** – The significance or purpose that gives value to actions and experiences.

Example – Choosing a career that aligns with your values creates meaning in your work.

16.   **Mental Toughness** – The ability to stay strong, focused, and resilient under pressure.

Example – Staying calm and performing well during a high-stakes presentation demonstrates mental toughness.

17. **Modesty** – Having a humble view of one's importance or achievements.

Example – Accepting praise graciously while acknowledging team contributions shows modesty.

18. **Mindset** – The established set of attitudes held by someone that shapes behavior and perception.

Example – Approaching challenges with a growth-oriented mindset encourages learning and resilience.

19. **Meal Planning:** Organizing meals ahead of time to support health and nutrition goals.

Example – Preparing lunches for the week in advance is meal planning that helps maintain healthy eating habits.

14

N

1. **Narrative Identity:** The story you tell yourself about who you are.

   Example – Viewing yourself as a lifelong learner becomes part of your narrative identity and influences your actions.

2. **Networking:** Building, Interacting, and maintaining relationships exchanging information and developing contacts for mutual support and opportunities .

   Example – Attending professional events and staying in touch with peers demonstrates effective networking.

3. **Net Worth:** The total assets minus total liabilities of an individual

   Example – Calculating your net worth by adding savings, investments, and property value and subtracting debts shows your financial position.

4. **Nutrition** – The process of providing or obtaining the food necessary for health and growth.

   Example – Eating balanced meals with adequate protein, healthy fats, and vegetables supports optimal nutrition.

5. **Neuroplasticity** – The brain's ability to reorganize and form new neural connections throughout life.

Example – Learning a new language strengthens brain pathways, illustrating neuroplasticity.

6. **Nonjudgment** – An attitude of openness and acceptance without criticism or evaluation.

Example – Listening to someone's perspective without immediately labeling it right or wrong shows nonjudgment.

7. **Nimbleness** – Quickness and agility in thought or movement.

Example – Adapting instantly to a sudden change in a project plan demonstrates mental nimbleness.

8. **Needs Assessment** – The process of identifying gaps between current and desired conditions.

Example – Evaluating your skills before starting a new job helps identify areas for development in a needs assessment.

9. **Narrative** – The structured story you tell about yourself or your experiences.

Example – Writing a reflection about a life-changing event creates a personal narrative.

10. **Nutrient Density:** Amount of beneficial nutrients in a food relative to its calorie content.

Example – Eating spinach, which is high in vitamins but low in calories, reflects a nutrient-dense choice.

11. **Negotiation** – The process of reaching a mutually acceptable agreement through communication.

Example – Discussing a fair salary during a job offer is a form of negotiation.

12. **Novelty** – The quality of being new or unusual, often sparking creativity and interest.

Example – Trying a new hobby like painting introduces novelty into your routine.

13. **Nurturing** – Providing care and encouragement to foster growth and development.

Example – Mentoring a junior colleague to help them succeed demonstrates nurturing.

15

O

1. **Ownership:** Taking full responsibility for your thoughts, actions, decisions, and their outcomes.

   Example – Accepting responsibility for a missed deadline at work instead of blaming others demonstrates ownership.

2. **Opportunity** – A favorable set of circumstances that allows for progress or advancement.

   Example – Attending a networking event that connects you with potential collaborators is an opportunity.

3. **Optimism** – A hopeful and positive outlook toward the future.

   Example – Believing you can recover from a setback and continue pursuing goals reflects optimism.

4. **Observation** – The active noticing and attention to details in your environment or behavior.

   Example – Watching how colleagues respond in meetings helps improve your own communication through observation.

5. **Openness** – Willingness to consider new ideas, experiences, and perspectives.

Example – Trying a new approach to solving a problem shows openness to innovation.

6. **Outcome** – The result or consequence of an action or decision.

Example – Completing a project successfully is a positive outcome of careful planning and execution.

7. **Overcoming** – Successfully dealing with challenges or obstacles.

Example – Learning to manage anxiety before public speaking demonstrates overcoming personal obstacles.

8. **Orderliness** – A systematic and organized approach to tasks and life.

Example – Keeping your workspace clean and prioritizing tasks daily reflects orderliness.

9. **Originality** – The ability to create unique ideas or approaches.

Example – Designing a marketing campaign with a completely new concept shows originality.

10. **Objectivity** – The quality of being unbiased and impartial in judgment.

Example – Evaluating a situation based on evidence rather than personal feelings demonstrates objectivity.

16

P

1.   **Paradigm:** A framework of beliefs and assumptions shaping how you see the world.

Example – Believing success comes only from formal education reflects a specific paradigm about achievement.

2.   **Perception:** How you interpret information and events.

Example – Viewing constructive criticism as an opportunity to improve shows a positive perception.

3.   **Personal Branding:** Marketing yourself and your career as a brand.

Example – Sharing your expertise on social media to build a professional reputation is personal branding.

4.   **Pitch Deck:** Brief presentation used to provide an overview of a business plan.

Example – Entrepreneurs use a pitch deck to present their startup concept to investors.

5.   **Perspective:** A particular attitude or way of viewing something.

Example – Looking at failure as a learning opportunity demonstrates a growth perspective.

6. **Passive Income:** Money earned with minimal activity through investments or side ventures.

Example – Earning rent from a property or dividends from stocks is a form of passive income.

7. **Purpose** – A sense of meaningful direction that motivates your actions and decisions.

Example – Choosing a career in education because you want to help others learn reflects purpose.

8. **Persistence** – Continued effort toward a goal despite difficulties or delays.

Example – Practicing daily for months to master a skill demonstrates persistence.

9. **Patience** – The capacity to accept or tolerate delay, trouble, or suffering without frustration.

Example – Waiting calmly for results after submitting a job application shows patience.

10. **Passion** – Intense enthusiasm or strong desire for something meaningful.

Example – Spending hours painting because it brings joy and purpose reflects passion.

11.   **Positivity** – The practice of focusing on the good aspects and maintaining an optimistic outlook.

Example – Reframing challenges as opportunities is an example of positivity in action.

12.   **Preparation** – The act of making ready for future events or challenges.

Example – Planning your study schedule before exams reflects preparation.

13.   **Perseverance** – Steadfastness in doing something despite difficulty or delay in achieving success

Example – Completing a marathon after months of training illustrates perseverance.

14.   **Productivity** – The efficiency of producing results and accomplishing goals.

Example – Using time blocks to complete work tasks increases productivity.

15.   **Progress** – Forward or onward movement toward a destination or goal.

Example – Improving your mile time each week reflects measurable progress.

16.   **Presence:** Being fully engaged in the current moment.

Example – Actively listening to a friend without distraction demonstrates presence.

17. **Progressive Overload:** Gradually increasing the stress placed on the body during training.

   Example – Adding more weight to your lifts each week represents progressive overload.

18. **Personal Mission Statement:** Statement of an individual's core purpose and focus in life.

   Example – Writing "To empower others through education and mentorship" as a personal mission statement guides your actions.

19. **Probiotics:** Live beneficial bacteria that promote gut health.

   Example – Consuming yogurt with live cultures introduces probiotics into your diet.

20. **Preventive Health:** Actions taken to prevent diseases rather than treating them.

   Example – Regular exercise and annual checkups demonstrate preventive health practices.

21. **Periodization:** Planned variation in training to optimize performance and recovery.

   Example – Cycling through strength, endurance, and recovery phases in a workout plan illustrates periodization.

17

Q

1. **Quality** – The standard of something as measured against other things; degree of excellence.

    Example – Producing well-researched work consistently reflects high quality.

2. **Questioning** – The practice of asking questions to deepen understanding and challenge assumptions.

    Example – Asking "Why does this happen?" when learning a new concept demonstrates questioning.

3. **Quietude** – A state of calmness and tranquility, important for reflection and mindfulness.

    Example – Sitting in a quiet park for 10 minutes each morning promotes quietude.

4. **Quitting (Healthy)** – Choosing to stop behaviors or situations that no longer serve your growth.

    Example – Leaving a toxic relationship or unfulfilling job reflects healthy quitting.

5. **Quickness** – The ability to think or respond rapidly and effectively.

    Example – Quickly solving a problem during a high-pressure meeting shows mental quickness.

6. **Quest** – A purposeful search or pursuit of personal or professional goals.

    Example – Training for a marathon as a personal challenge represents a quest.

7. **Quotient** – A measure or degree of a particular quality or characteristic (e.g., emotional quotient).

    Example – Emotional quotient (EQ) measures one's ability to understand and manage emotions.

8. **Quiescence** – A state of inactivity or rest that supports recovery and reflection.

    Example – Taking a day off to meditate and recharge exemplifies quiescence.

9. **Qualification** – A skill or attribute that makes you suitable for a particular role or task.

    Example – Earning a certification in project management is a qualification for leading projects.

10.   **Quench** – To satisfy or relieve a need, desire, or thirst, such as for knowledge or motivation.

Example – Reading an insightful book to learn a new skill helps quench intellectual curiosity.

18

R

1. **Reality:** The state of things as they actually exist, often filtered by beliefs and perception.

   Example – Accepting feedback from a colleague as it is, rather than how you fear it might be, reflects a clear view of reality.

2. **Resilience:** Capacity and ability to recover quickly from difficulties bounce back and adapt to adversity and failure.

   Example – Continuing to pursue goals after a setback demonstrates resilience.

3. **Reflection** – The process of thoughtfully considering your experiences and actions.

   Example – Journaling about a challenging week to understand what worked and what didn't is reflection.

4. **Responsibility** – Being accountable for your choices and their consequences.

   Example – Admitting a mistake at work and taking steps to correct it reflects responsibility.

5. **Respect** – Valuing yourself and others through recognition and consideration.

Example – Listening actively without interrupting demonstrates respect in communication.

6. **Risk-taking** – The willingness to face uncertainty for potential growth or reward.

    Example – Starting a new business venture despite uncertainty illustrates risk-taking.

7. **Restoration** – The process of renewal and healing after stress or hardship.

    Example – Taking a weekend retreat to recharge and reset represents restoration.

8. **Routine** – A regular sequence of actions or habits that support your goals.

    Example – Morning meditation followed by exercise forms a daily wellness routine.

9. **Recognition** – Acknowledging achievements, strengths, or contributions.

    Example – Praising a teammate for their hard work shows recognition.

10. **Readiness** – Being prepared mentally, emotionally, or physically to take action.

    Example – Practicing emergency drills ensures readiness in unex-

pected situations.

11. **Reframing** – Changing your perspective or how you see a situation to see it more positively or constructively.

   Example – Seeing a failed project as a learning opportunity rather than a loss demonstrates reframing.

19

S

1.   **Self-actualization**: the process of realizing and fulfilling your highest potential, becoming the most authentic, capable, and complete version of yourself. It's the peak of personal development where your actions align with your values, passions, and purpose, becoming who you're truly meant to be—growing into your best self in every area of life.

Example – Choosing a career that aligns with your passions and values while continuing personal growth reflects self-actualization.

2.   **Stamina** – The physical or mental endurance to sustain prolonged effort or activity.

Example – Running a marathon or staying focused on a long-term project demonstrates stamina.

3.   **Strategy** – A plan of action designed to achieve a long-term goal.

Example – Creating a study schedule to complete a certification program illustrates strategy.

4.   **Synergy** – The combined effect that exceeds the sum of individual efforts.

Example – A team working together to innovate a product demon-

strates synergy.

5.   **Support** – Assistance or encouragement to help someone grow or overcome challenges.

Example – Mentoring a junior colleague to help them improve skills is providing support.

6.   **Sacrifice** – Giving up something valuable for the sake of a greater goal or benefit.

Example – Studying instead of going out with friends to achieve a career goal is a sacrifice.

7.   **Strength** – The quality of being strong physically, mentally, or emotionally.

Example – Maintaining composure and focus under pressure demonstrates mental strength.

8.   **Stillness** – A state of calm and quiet that fosters mindfulness and reflection.

Example – Sitting quietly for meditation to regain focus reflects stillness.

9.   **Sincerity** – Genuine honesty and openness in thoughts and actions.

Example – Giving honest feedback while being empathetic demonstrates sincerity.

10. **Spontaneity** – Acting on impulse or natural feeling without overthinking.

Example – Taking an unplanned trip to explore a new place shows spontaneity.

11. **Success** – The achievement of a desired goal or outcome.

Example – Completing a long-term project on time and exceeding expectations represents success.

12. **Self-Directed Learning:** Taking initiative and responsibility for one's own learning.

Example – Learning a new programming language by following online tutorials independently demonstrates self-directed learning.

13. **Scaffolding:** Support given to learners to promote independent learning.

Example – A teacher breaking a complex task into manageable steps is using scaffolding.

14. **Self-Awareness:** Recognizing & Understanding your own emotions, thoughts, and behaviors.

Example – Noticing that stress makes you procrastinate reflects self-awareness.

15. **Self-Discipline:** Ability to control impulses and stay consistent with goals.

Example – Waking up early daily to exercise despite feeling tired shows self-discipline.

16.   **Self-Image:** How you see yourself—mentally, emotionally, and physically.

Example – Seeing yourself as capable and confident reflects a positive self-image.

17.   **Self-Efficacy:** Belief in one's ability to succeed in specific situations.

Example – Feeling confident you can complete a challenging project reflects self-efficacy.

18.   **Self-Mastery:** Control over your thoughts, emotions, and habits.

Example – Managing anger and responding thoughtfully in conflicts demonstrates self-mastery.

19.   **Self-Perception:** How you view your own strengths, weaknesses, and worth.

Example – Recognizing your creativity and areas to improve reflects accurate self-perception

20.   **Self-Talk:** The internal voice that narrates your life and influences self-esteem.

Example – Encouraging yourself before a presentation demonstrates positive self-talk.

21.   **Self-Worth:** Your internal sense of value and self-respect.

Example – Standing up for your needs in a relationship reflects healthy self-worth.

22.   **Self-Reflection:** Analyzing your actions and experiences to foster personal growth.

Example – Reviewing your performance after a project to identify improvements is self-reflection.

23.   **Sleep Hygiene:** Habits and practices that are conducive to sleeping well on a regular basis.

Example – Keeping a consistent bedtime and limiting screens before bed promotes good sleep hygiene.

24.   **Stress Management:** Techniques and therapies to control a person's level of stress.

Example – Practicing deep breathing or meditation to manage work stress reflects stress management.

25.   **Subconscious Programming:** Automatic thought patterns formed through experience and repetition.

Example – Reacting with fear to public speaking due to past negative experiences reflects subconscious programming.

26.   **Supplementation:** Using vitamins, minerals, or other nutrients to enhance diet.

Example – Taking vitamin D during winter months to maintain health is supplementation.

20 |

T

1.   **Time Management:** The skill of organizing and planning how to divide your time effectively.

Example – Using a daily planner to schedule work, exercise, and personal tasks demonstrates time management.

2.   **Transcendence:** Rising above limiting beliefs or ego to achieve growth.

Example – Letting go of fear of failure to pursue your dreams reflects transcendence.

3.   **Transmutation:** Transforming negative energy or emotion into growth or creativity.

Example – Channeling frustration from a setback into motivation to improve demonstrates transmutation.

4.   **Time Blocking:** Scheduling specific periods for different activities to increase efficiency. The action to enhance time management.

Example – Blocking 9–11 AM for deep work and 2–3 PM for meetings illustrates time blocking.

5. **Tenacity** – Persistent determination to keep going despite obstacles.

    Example – Practicing a difficult skill daily until mastery shows tenacity.

6. **Transformation** – A profound change in form, mindset, or behavior.

    Example – Overhauling your health habits to achieve lasting wellness reflects transformation.

7. **Trust** – Confidence in the reliability, truth, or ability of someone or something.

    Example – Relying on a teammate to complete their part of a project demonstrates trust.

8. **Truth** – Conformity to fact or reality; honesty in thoughts and actions.

    Example – Admitting a mistake at work instead of covering it up demonstrates truth.

9. **Tolerance** – Acceptance and open-mindedness toward differences and challenges.

    Example – Respecting diverse opinions in a discussion reflects tolerance.

10. **Teamwork** – Collaborative effort toward shared goals.

    Example – Coordinating with colleagues to complete a group project demonstrates teamwork.

11.   **Thoughtfulness** – Consideration for others and careful reflection.

Example – Checking in on a friend going through a difficult time shows thoughtfulness.

12.   **Training** – The process of developing skills or knowledge through practice.

Example – Attending weekly workshops to improve public speaking represents training.

13. **Transition** – The process of changing from one state or condition to another.

Example – Shifting from a student lifestyle to a professional career reflects a major life transition.

21

U

1. **Understanding** – The ability to grasp the meaning or significance of something.

   Example – Explaining a complex concept clearly to someone else demonstrates understanding.

2. **Unity** – A state of harmony and agreement within oneself or among people.

   Example – A team working together without conflict toward a shared goal reflects unity.

3. **Unlearning** – The process of letting go of outdated or unhelpful knowledge and habits.

   Example – Relearning a more effective way to manage time demonstrates unlearning old habits.

4. **Urgency** – A sense of importance and promptness in taking action.

   Example – Responding immediately to a critical issue at work shows urgency.

5. **Usefulness** – The quality of being practical and beneficial for achieving goals.

Example – Choosing tools and strategies that actually help you accomplish tasks reflects usefulness.

6. **Upliftment** – The act of raising spirits, motivation, or status.

Example – Encouraging a friend to keep pursuing their goals demonstrates upliftment.

7. **Unwavering** – Steadfast and resolute in purpose or belief.

Example – Continuing to work toward a long-term goal despite setbacks shows unwavering dedication.

8. **Uniqueness** – The quality of being one-of-a-kind, distinct from others.

Example – Using your personal perspective to solve a problem creatively highlights uniqueness.

9. **Upward Mobility** – The ability to improve one's social or economic status.

Example – Pursuing education and skill development to earn a higher-paying job illustrates upward mobility.

10. **Utilization** – Making effective use of resources, skills, or opportunities.

Example – Applying learned techniques from a workshop directly to your work demonstrates proper utilization.

22

V

1.   **Visualization:** Creating a mental image or imagining success to reinforce belief and motivation to increase the likelihood of a desired outcome or performance

Example – Visualizing yourself delivering a successful presentation before the event demonstrates visualization.

2.   **Values Clarification:** Identifying which values and what is most important to guide decision-making.

Example – Determining that integrity and family come first in life decisions reflects values clarification.

3.   **Vision** – A clear, inspiring picture of the future you want to create.

Example – Setting a long-term goal to start your own business reflects having a vision.

4.   **Values** – Core principles and beliefs that guide your decisions and behavior.

Example – Honesty and compassion guiding your actions reflects your personal values.

5. **Vitality** – The state of being strong, active, and full of energy.

   Example – Maintaining energy to work, exercise, and enjoy life reflects vitality.

6. **Validation** – Recognizing and affirming your feelings, experiences, or achievements.

   Example – Telling a friend their feelings are understandable demonstrates validation.

7. **Vulnerability** – The willingness to be open and authentic, despite potential risks.

   Example – Sharing personal struggles with a trusted colleague shows vulnerability.

8. **Versatility** – The ability to adapt easily to different situations or tasks.

   Example – Switching between different roles in a project seamlessly demonstrates versatility.

9. **Victory** – The achievement of success or overcoming obstacles.

   Example – Completing a challenging marathon or project represents victory.

10. **Volition** – The power of choosing or deciding; willpower.

    Example – Choosing to wake up early to study despite feeling tired demonstrates volition.

11. **Value Creation** – The process of producing something beneficial or meaningful.

*Example – Developing a product that solves a common problem ex-
emplifies value creation.*

23

W

1. **Wellness:** The active process and pursuit of becoming aware of and making choices toward a healthy balance in body, mind, and spirit creating a fulfilling life.

    Example – Regular exercise, mindful eating, and stress management practices reflect wellness.

2. **Whole Foods:** Foods that are minimally processed and close to their natural form.

    Example – Fresh fruits, vegetables, and unprocessed grains are considered whole foods.

3. **Wisdom** – The ability to apply knowledge and experience with good judgment.

    Example – Advising someone based on past experiences rather than just theory demonstrates wisdom.

4. **Willpower** – The inner strength to control impulses and stay focused on goals.

    Example – Resisting the urge to skip workouts demonstrates willpower.

5. **Work Ethic** – A commitment to doing your best work consistently.

    Example – Arriving early, being prepared, and completing tasks thoroughly shows strong work ethic.

6. **Worthiness** – A sense of being deserving of good things and respect.

    Example – Recognizing that you deserve success and self-care reflects worthiness.

7. **Willingness** – Openness and readiness to take on challenges or change.

    Example – Volunteering for a challenging project demonstrates willingness.

8. **Wonder** – A feeling of awe and curiosity about the world.

    Example – Exploring a new culture or nature trail evokes a sense of wonder.

9. **Winning** – Achieving success or reaching desired outcomes.

    Example – Completing a challenging project successfully represents winning.

10. **Wisdom Sharing** – The act of passing on knowledge and lessons learned to others.

    Example – Mentoring a junior colleague reflects wisdom sharing.

24

X

1.   **X-factor** – An outstanding special quality or talent that sets someone apart.

     Example – A speaker's charisma that captivates an audience demonstrates their X-factor.

2.   **Xenial** – Showing hospitality and kindness toward strangers or guests.

     Example – Welcoming a new neighbor with a homemade meal demonstrates xenial behavior.

3.   **Xenodochy** – The act of welcoming and caring for strangers or newcomers.

     Example – Providing resources and support to new employees shows xenodochy.

4.   **Xenophilia** – An attraction to or love of foreign cultures and ideas.

     Example – Studying international art and traditions demonstrates xenophilia.

5.   **Xenogenesis** – The creation of something new or different from what previously existed.

Example – Developing a completely new approach to a problem represents xenogenesis.

6. **Xylography** – (Metaphorically) The art of carving out your own path or legacy.

   Example – Starting a movement that impacts your community demonstrates xylography.

7. **Xerophilous** – Thriving or growing in dry or challenging conditions (used metaphorically for resilience).

   Example – Maintaining optimism and productivity despite adversity shows a xerophilous mindset.

8. **Xenotropic** – Adapting to or thriving in new or foreign environments.

   Example – Excelling in a new country or culture reflects xenotropic qualities.

9. **Xyloid** – Having qualities of strength and endurance, like wood (used metaphorically).

   Example – Staying grounded and persistent through challenges demonstrates a xyloid nature.

10. **X-factor Mindset** – A mindset that embraces uniqueness, innovation, and distinction

    Example – Approaching problems with creativity and confidence in your originality reflects an X-factor mindset.

25

Y

1. **Yearning** – A strong desire or longing for growth, purpose, or connection.

    Example – Feeling motivated to pursue a new skill or career reflects yearning.

2. **Yielding** – The ability to adapt or give way without losing strength or purpose.

    Example – Adjusting plans when unexpected challenges arise demonstrates yielding.

3. **Youthfulness** – A mindset or quality of being energetic, open, and curious.

    Example – Approaching new experiences with curiosity and excitement shows youthfulness.

4. **Yes-mindedness** – Openness to new experiences and positive opportunities.

    Example – Saying "yes" to a challenging project to learn new skills reflects yes-mindedness.

5. **Yin-Yang** – The concept of balance and harmony between opposing forces.

Example – Balancing work and rest to maintain well-being embodies yin-yang principles.

6. **Yoke** – Symbolic connection or partnership that supports mutual growth.

Example – Collaborating with a mentor to achieve shared goals reflects a yoke.

7. **Yoga** – A practice that unites body, mind, and spirit for holistic well-being.

Example – Practicing daily yoga to reduce stress and increase focus reflects holistic care.

8. **Year-round Growth** – Consistent development and improvement throughout all seasons of life.

Example – Continuously reading, learning, and refining skills demonstrates year-round growth.

9. **Yield** – The positive results or benefits gained from efforts and investments.

Example – Completing a project successfully after months of work reflects yield.

10. **Youth Empowerment** – Encouraging and supporting young people to develop confidence and skills.

Example – Mentoring teenagers to explore career opportunities demonstrates youth empowerment.

26

Z

1. **Zeal** – Great enthusiasm and passion for a cause or goal.

    Example – Approaching every task with excitement and dedication reflects zeal.

2. **Zen** – A state of calm attentiveness and mindfulness.

    Example – Meditating daily to maintain mental clarity embodies Zen.

3. **Zest** – Energetic enjoyment and enthusiasm for life.

    Example – Approaching challenges with optimism and excitement reflects zest.

4. **Zone** – A mental state of focused immersion and peak performance.

    Example – Being completely absorbed in creative work demonstrates being in the zone.

5. **Zero-based Thinking** – A mindset of re-evaluating decisions as if starting fresh from zero.

    Example – Considering whether to continue a project from scratch demonstrates zero-based thinking.

6. **Zigzag Learning** – Learning that happens in non-linear, dynamic ways.

    Example – Exploring different subjects, experimenting, and looping back to concepts reflects zigzag learning.

7. **Zooming Out** – Stepping back to see the bigger picture for better perspective.

    Example – Reviewing overall goals before focusing on small tasks demonstrates zooming out.

8. **Zephyr** – A gentle breeze symbolizing ease and flow in life.

    Example – Approaching tasks with calmness and adaptability reflects zephyr energy.

9. **Zenith** – The highest point of achievement or development.

    Example – Completing a lifelong goal or reaching peak performance reflects zenith.

10. **Zealousness** – Fervent dedication and eagerness to pursue growth.

    Example – Consistently putting effort into personal mastery shows zealousness.

CONCLUSION

Being CZND means living in a state of *deep alignment* with your purpose, grounded in *mastery, confidence, awareness,* and *action*. It represents a lifestyle of intentional growth where you are actively realizing your potential and embodying your highest self.

To be CZND is to operate from clarity—not chaos. It's when your thoughts, choices, energy, and goals are connected, deliberate, and empowering. You are not reacting to life—you are leading it.

In essence: Being CZND is *being locked in*, fully present, and fully expressed in who you are and who you are becoming.

SuperCZND is the *elevated expression* of being CZND—it's when alignment turns into momentum, and mastery becomes lifestyle. It represents *peak awareness, embodied power, limitless mindset,* and *purpose-driven impact*.

SuperCZND isn't just about becoming your best—it's about **living from that place consistently**, leading others, breaking limits, and rewriting what's possible for your life and legacy.

In essence: SuperCZND is your **unapologetic greatness in motion**—where vision, voice, and values are not just aligned, but unstoppable.

SuperCZND & Ultra Instinct: The Parallel of Mastery in Motion

SuperCZND, like **Ultra Instinct**, represents a transcendent state of being—one where action flows without hesitation, and intention aligns perfectly with execution. It's not just power or potential—it's the mastery of self to the point where **thinking and doing become one seamless motion**.

In **Dragon Ball Super**, Goku enters Ultra Instinct only after intense challenge, inner stillness, and full surrender to the moment. It's a form where his body reacts *without the interference of doubt, fear, or overthinking*. Every movement is instinctive, precise, and aligned with purpose.

That is **SuperCZND**:
When you're no longer *trying* to be confident—you *are* confidence. When awareness and action are no longer separate—they are *synchronized*. When your lifestyle isn't about chasing growth—it *embodies* it. When you're *so aligned*, the world around you bends to meet your energy.

Like Goku in Ultra Instinct, **SuperCZND is your highest self activated**—calm yet powerful, still yet strategic, present yet always evolving. It's self-mastery without force. Clarity without confusion. Movement without resistance.

SuperCZND = Ultra Instinct for real life:
When your mindset, mission, and motion are fully harmonized, and your presence becomes your power.

Conclusion: The Vocabulary of Your Becoming
Your journey of self-mastery doesn't end with the final word—it begins with how you choose to live the definitions you've just discovered.

The terms in this book are not just knowledge to absorb, but wisdom to apply. Each one is a stepping stone toward deeper self-awareness, stronger habits, healthier choices, more confident decisions, and a more intentional lifestyle.

Growth happens in moments—moments when you remember what discipline means, when you choose resilience over reaction, or when you re-frame your challenges through the lens of possibility. These words are tools for those moments.

Revisit this dictionary often. Let it grow with you. Let it challenge and refine you. Use it as a compass when you're uncertain and as fuel when you're ready to rise. Because your language shapes your life—and now, you have the vocabulary to shape it on purpose.

Keep learning. Keep evolving. Keep becoming.

LIVING ALIGNED & BECOMING CZND

www.ingramcontent.com/pod-product-compliance
Lightning Source LLC
Chambersburg PA
CBHW031131020426

42333CB00012B/326